GENEVIEVE

A LOVE STORY

Acknowledgement

This book would not exist at all had it not been for my wife Joan. While my salary supported us, her teaching paid for Genevieve!

In the book, which spans twenty plus years, I have tried to be as accurate with regard to dates and events as possible. Fortunately Joan is a hoarder and thanks to this she was able by means of old menus, receipts, match books, back issues of the Ontario Jaguar Owners Assn., etc., etc., to put the events prior to the repurchasing of Genevieve in good order.

While the book does not contain a great deal of text, nonetheless, many hours were spent reviewing and discussing each page. This Joan and I did together, after which I'd generally have to rewrite each one!

Not the least of her contributions was enduring the mental anguish of seeing all that money 'flying out the window' during Genevieve's restoration.

ISBN 0 85429 362 0

A FOULIS Motoring Book

This edition first published 1983

Reprinted 1983

Published by:
Haynes Publishing Group
Sparkford, Yeovil, Somerset BA22 7JJ, England

Distributed in North America by:
Haynes Publications Inc.
861 Lawrence Drive, Newbury Park,
California 91320, USA

Editor: Rod Grainger
Page layout: Lynne Blackburn &
Sandra Whitaker

Printed in England, by: J. H. Haynes & Co. Ltd

Foulis

Haynes

GENEVIEVE

A LOVE STORY

Seldom, if ever, do I set my alarm for 6.30 am on a holiday morning, but this was a very special holiday indeed. It was Memorial Day Monday May 31, 1976, the day on which I would see Genevieve for the first time in five years.

I'd been plain dumb to sell her in the first place. Joan, my wife, told me I'd be sorry, and she was right. At first I hadn't missed Genevieve too much but, as time passed, I began to remember what a beautiful automobile she had been and the many years of fun we had shared – however, more about that later ....

I dressed, hurried down stairs, grabbed a quick breakfast, grabbed my cameras and headed for the garage.

It was a beautiful spring day, perfect convertible weather. I folded down the car's top and backed out of the driveway of my home in Park Ridge, Illinois. Five minutes later I turned left onto the highway and headed south towards Laporte, a small town in north-eastern Indiana. I had driven this route dozens of times in Genevieve, back and forth from Toronto. Soon the familiar communications tower near the Laporte exit appeared on the horizon. I swung off onto Route 35 – Genevieve's present owner had told me his home was about a mile from the highway and to look for a freshly laid stone driveway. Due to the abnormal amount of rain the past week, he asked if I'd park at the base of the drive. Of course I would.

A few minutes after leaving the highway I was there. It was a long driveway and, at the end, off to one side, I could see her! Genevieve was indeed every bit as beautiful an automobile as I had remembered.

For a few minutes, I just sat in my car and stared. I could tell, even at sixty yards or so, that she needed a good waxing but that was of little concern. I hopped out and started walking towards her to get a better look. I remember I was smiling as I approached but my smile began to fade the closer I got ....

Genevieve ... *Oh,* Genevieve! Our beautiful automobile was a battered hulk of rotted, rusting steel and pitted chrome, parked there in the weeds, her bald tyres caked with mud. I simply could not believe what my eyes were seeing.

The body in front of the left front wheel was badly smashed, and the two doors on the left hand side had a deep crease along their bottoms. Inside, the once magnificent burled walnut instrument panel and window ledges were a wreck. Exposure to the elements had seen to that. The Connolly leather seats were dried out and brittle to the touch. I walked around her several times looking at the badly pitted chrome that had once reflected the approving faces of *Concours d'Elegance* judges. I shuddered each time I saw more rust and rotted out steel. The chrome trim around the back window had separated, lights were broken, hub caps missing ... what a horrible sight! Finally I opened the door, brushed away a grasshopper and sat down.

Behind the wheel again, my thoughts drifted back to a cold December night in 1959 ....

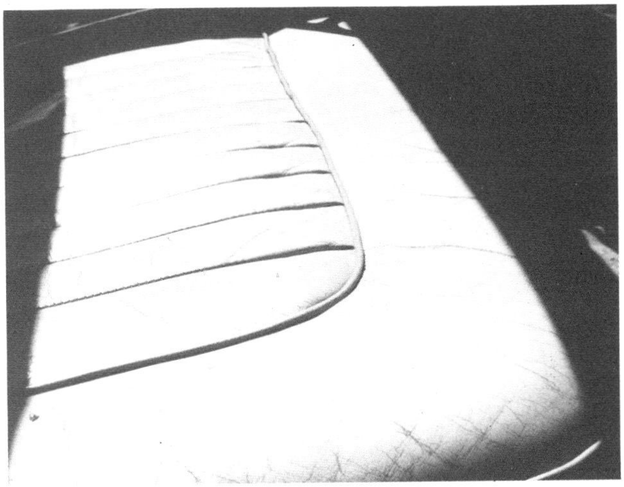

My seventy year young, two Martinis a night, Aunt Mary had come to spend the weekend with us in Highland Park. We were having our first Martini when the call came. Our new Jaguar Mk IX was ready for collection. Originally the car was to have been delivered to Navy Pier in Chicago, via the St.Lawrence Seaway. There had, however, been a misunderstanding as to the interior colour which caused a three month delay. We had ordered a tan interior and, fortunately in time, had found out that in the UK tan is brown, and biscuit is tan. By mid-December the Seaway had frozen over. We were not about to wait for it to thaw.

The three of us arrived early the following morning at O'Hare International Airport and boarded a United Airlines jet to New York.

We took a taxi from Kennedy International Airport, New York, straight to the garage on the Avenue of the Americas. She was even more beautiful that we had imagined. We had seen a lot of Mk IXs before we decided to buy one, but never in 'our' colour combination: British Racing Green with the 'tan' interior. After half an hour of *oohing* and *aahing* and some necessary paperwork, we headed for the Beekman Tower Hotel where we planned to spend a few days before heading home. I remember that when we got there, the doorman wouldn't let me park the Jaguar in the regular garage used by the hotel. Instead he found her a spot in a private garage over on Sutton Place. She was in fine company over there with the many, and I mean *many,* Rolls-Royces and Bentleys. That evening, in the roof top lounge at Beekman Tower, over a glass of champagne, we christened her 'Genevieve II'.

We spent several fun days in Manhattan, then drove Genevieve home, resplendent with her British number plates.

Slipping back a little further in time, I should explain that our interest in the wonderful world of exotic automobiles had begun shortly after Joan and I were married. One couple we knew had a little white MG TD sports car. Another couple in the neighbourhood owned a 1924 Bentley and together, we were all active in a number of classic automobile events. Still another friend bought one of the first Volkswagens imported to the United States. He participated in rallies nearly every weekend. It was all so much fun that we thought we should get a classic of our own. We bought the tomato red Jaguar XK120 you see here. We named her 'Genevieve' after the then popular movie about the British London to Brighton race. From then on we were active in lots of events with our own car.

Two weekends each year, a group of us would head up to Elkhart Lake, Wisconsin, to watch the Sports Car Club of America June Sprints and, later in the season, the Road America 500 Race. We had a favourite spot, just north of Milwaukee, where we'd all meet for a picnic and then push on to Rutherfords Motel on Lake Michigan – a short drive from the track.

During the winter there were ice races on Lake Geneva, again in Wisconsin, and always the weekend rallies.

Even for a young couple with no children, one car, as cramped as Genevieve, was a bit inconvenient, so we reluctantly made up our minds to sell her and get a bigger car. I don't believe it had any bearing on our decision to sell, but I do remember the many evenings my wife would arrive at the Highland Park train station to pick me up and it would start to rain. The roof, which had to be raised by hand, was impossible for one gal to operate and so she would sit there in the rain muttering, 'I am a sport! I *am* a sport! ... *I am a sport?*'

We saw an ad for the new Jaguar Mk IX in *Road & Track* magazine and that settled it.

Now, Genevieve II was no wind-in-the-hair sports car, but we decided to keep on rallying. We installed seat belts when Ralph Nader, the car safety expert, was still in knee pants and Genevieve became a competitor in the true Jaguar tradition. Pictured above is Genevieve in the Carson's British Fortnight Rallye and Gymkhana in October of 1961. The rallye started at the Carson Pirie Scott & Company department store in Chicago and ended at the gymkhana site, a racecourse in Wilmot, Illinois, about forty five miles north.

Incidentally, we dropped the designation 'II' shortly after getting our new Jaguar home from New York.

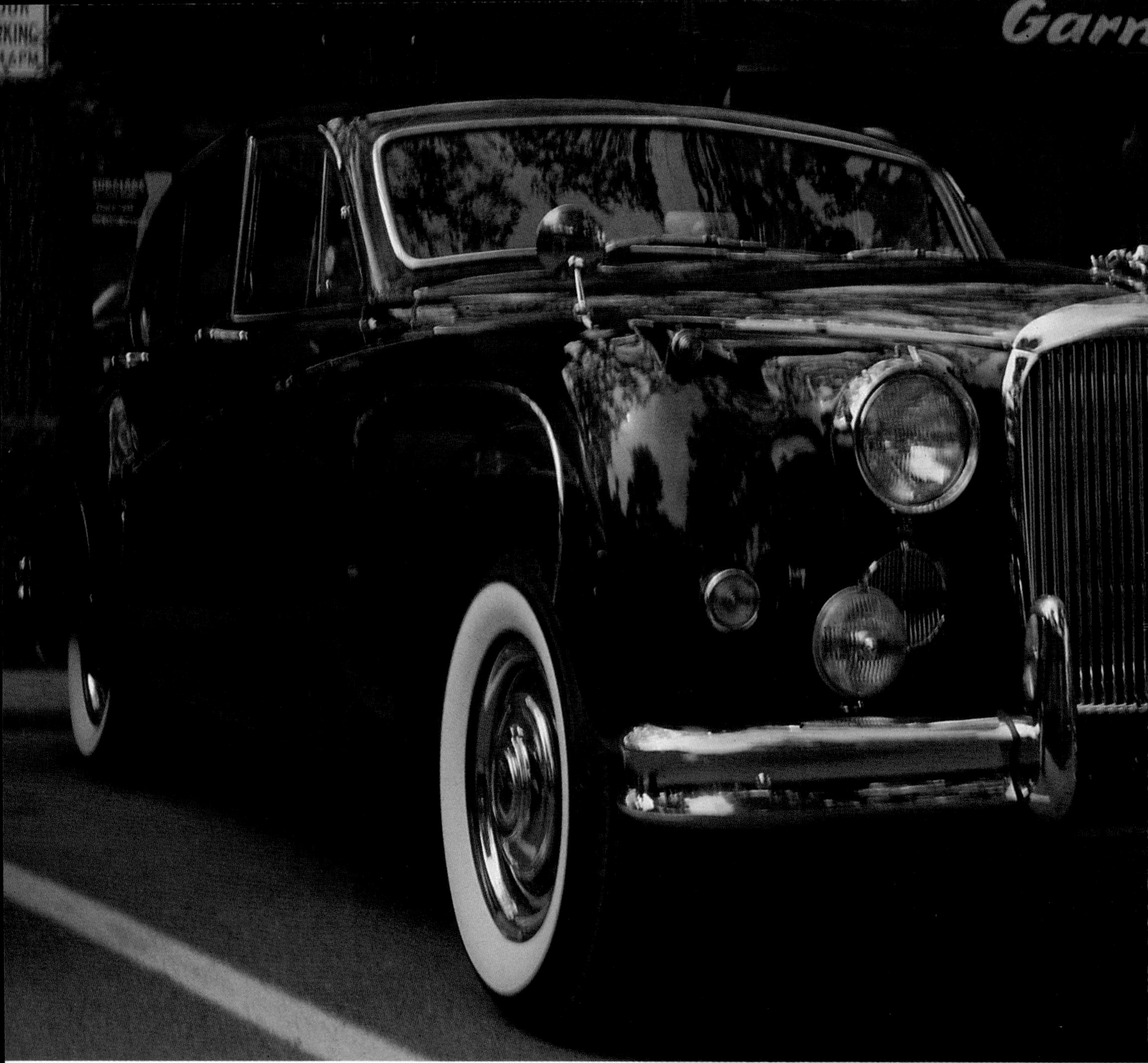

V. S. C. C.
Concourse on the Square
June 25, 1961
2nd

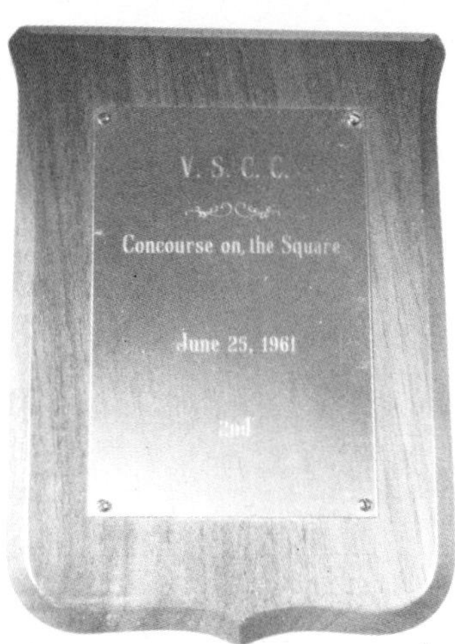

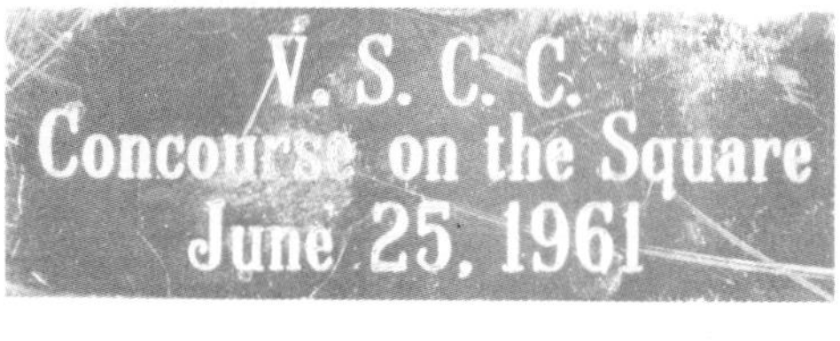
V. S. C. C.
Concourse on the Square
June 25, 1961

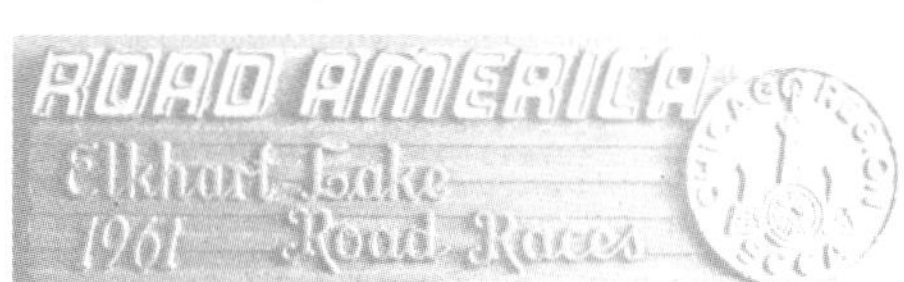

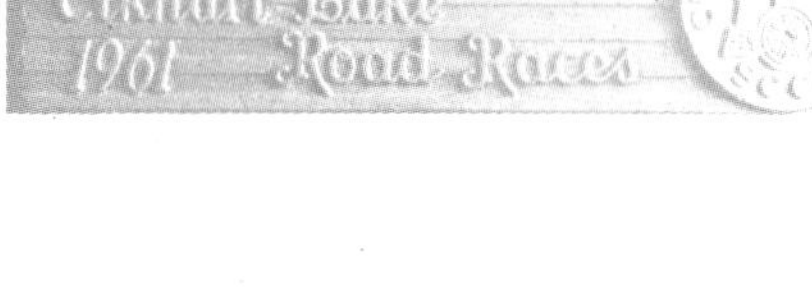
ROAD AMERICA
Elkhart Lake
1961 Road Races

Concurrent with the races at Elkhart Lake, Wisconsin, the Sports Car Club of America holds its annual mid-west region *Concours d'Elegance*. We decided to enter Genevieve in the 1961 event. This was a major *concours* and attracted magnificent automobiles from hundreds of miles around. We would be in competition with classic Rolls-Royces, Bentleys, Mercedes, MGs, Cords and dozens of other great marques.

At Rutherfords, during Friday afternoon, we washed and waxed Genevieve, vacuumed her interior and luggage compartment, and scrubbed the sidewalls of her large tyres to a dazzling white (Genevieve's original tyres were whitewalls, but all subsequent sets would be black).

Early Saturday morning we lined up with the other competitors. The engine was given a final polishing and the car dusted. We were ready by the 10.00 am deadline. Several teams, each of three judges, began meticulously examining each car. The results were to be announced that evening ....

Even though we had worked very hard preparing Genevieve, I really didn't think we had a chance, but, from the loudspeaker we heard: 'First in class is a beautiful Jaguar Mk IX owned by Mr. and Mrs. Smedley of Highland Park, Illinois.' My friends picked me up off the ground and we got in the car. Genevieve led the parade around the track that night to pick up her first place trophy – boy, was she proud!

June 25th of that year, we entered the Village Sports Car Club *Concours* held on the square in the town of Lake Forest, Illinois. Somewhere along the line we dropped a few points but finished a respectable second overall.

We missed a number of other events that year, for various reasons, and before we knew it the season was over.

Next year we planned to show Genevieve again. We would not. It would be the following year ... but not in the United States!

METROPOLITAN
TORONTO
POPULATION 1.595.800

In 1959, I had joined the Leo Burnett Company, an American advertising agency, as an art director. Late in the autumn of 1961, Howard Anderson, the head of the art department at the time, called me into his office. He wanted to know if I would be willing to go to the company's Toronto office to replace a chap who wished to come to the US office. You bet I would!

On New Year's Day of 1962 we crossed the border into Canada and headed up the Queens Highway 401 towards Toronto. Genevieve fairly bristled with pride as she swept along majestically.

During our first year in Canada we were so busy sightseeing and enjoying our new home, we didn't participate in any automobile related events.

The following year, however, we were at it again.

Alongside her Jaguar Clubs of North America badge, Genevieve now sported the badges of the Oakville-Trafalgar Light Car Club, The Ontario Jaguar Owners' Association and the Canadian Automobile Sports Club and a few others. The USA badge was a Christmas present from a doting Aunt Mary to Genevieve.

One of the first Canadian events in which we participated was The Canadian Winter Rally. I'd read about this event for years, and any rally enthusiast will tell you it's a 'biggie'. It may be the only rally on the North American Continent that attracts professional, factory-sponsored rally teams from the United States and Europe. Needless to say, we did not compete. The people who control the rally, manning the check points and so forth, are hand-picked by the Canadian Automobile Sports Club and we offered our services in whatever small capacity they might need. We were told to report to the garage area at North Bay, Ontario, the midway point of the rally.

The event began at 8.00 pm in Toronto. The starting line was ablaze with floodlights from the major television networks, punctuated by the strobe-lights of the press and magazine photographers – all very exciting!

When the the last car had left the starting line, Joan and I hopped into Genevieve and headed for North Bay, about 175 miles away and close to the border with Quebec. It was 20 degrees below zero when we arrived.

Joan was cold and tired and elected to sack out in the hotel room. I headed for the garage area. That night I was far from the most important member of the group but I'll wager I was the most popular. As the half-frozen drivers and navigators arrived, I performed the very important role of serving the hot coffee!

Dawn was breaking when I arrived back at the hotel. I grabbed a few hours of sleep. Late the next day we headed home to Toronto.

Maybe the rallies sponsored by the Oakville-Trafalgar Light Car Club didn't attract the television networks or other news media, but they were a lot of fun and if we didn't always compete we did at least assist by manning check points along the way.

One rally in which we did compete was The Tiny Tulip Rally in the Spring of 1963 – I'll never forget it. A great deal of snow had fallen that winter and at the time of the rally was in the process of melting. The rally route took us through very hilly country over dirt roads, still covered with snow for the most part, but not too bad. We were right on time, and on course, when we rounded a bend and approached a steep hill. It was a sheet of ice and fellow club members had spun out on both sides all the way up to the top. There was nothing to do but try it ourselves. I picked up as much speed as I could and started up. We nearly went into the ditch once but I regained control and kept going and as we neared the top, tyres struggling for grip, the ice began to disappear and the tyres suddenly dug in. We'd made it! We picked up speed rapidly and started down the other side ... the sunny side. To our horror, the road became a sea of mud and we literally slid down it, mud flying in all directions, and up to the axles in depth. When we finally got to the finish point, the front wheel wells were so caked with frozen mud, I could barely turn the steering wheel. We were among the few to finish that day!

That summer the Ontario Jaguar Owners Association along with the British Motor Industry held a *Concours* at the new Woodbine. As hard as we worked to get Genevieve in shape, we didn't even place. I think those rallies had taken their toll.

We had been competing and participating in various motoring events for nearly eight years and it was at this point our interest began to taper off. We continued to attend the meetings and social events but our competing days were at an end.

Genevieve retired to private life.

OAKVILLE-TRAFALGAR
LIGHT CAR CLUB
B.P.
ECONOMY RUN
1963

OAKVILLE-TRAFALGAR
LIGHT CAR CLUB
TINY TULIP RALLY
1963
OFFICIAL

OAKVILLE-TRAFALGAR
LIGHT CAR CLUB
MAY MAP RUN
1963
OFFICIAL

ONTARIO JAGUAR OWNERS
ASSOCIATION

OAKVILLE-TRAFALGAR
LIGHT CAR CLUB
CANADIAN AUTOMOBILE
SPORT CLUB

U.S.A

CANADA

I was working on a series of Kellogg's ads when a memo from Chicago came across my desk. Dick Weiner had been promoted to executive art director and was put in charge of the Schlitz Beer account. I had worked with Dick and liked him very much and so I decided to send him my congratulations but, rather than just a note, I decided to do something a little more personalized. I made a miniature billboard in the usual Schlitz advertisement format. I replaced the client's usual message with the word 'Congratulations' and lettered my name in the same style as the word 'Schlitz' that appears in the signature, or logotype. Two days later I got a call from Dick ... 'Come home!'

On Derby Day of 1964 we headed back down the Queens Highway 401 towards the USA and Chicago. Cruising along the highway we turned on the radio to listen to the Kentucky Derby. That day a Canadian horse named 'Northern Dancer' won the race. Somehow it seemed a fitting conclusion to our own northern caper in Canada.

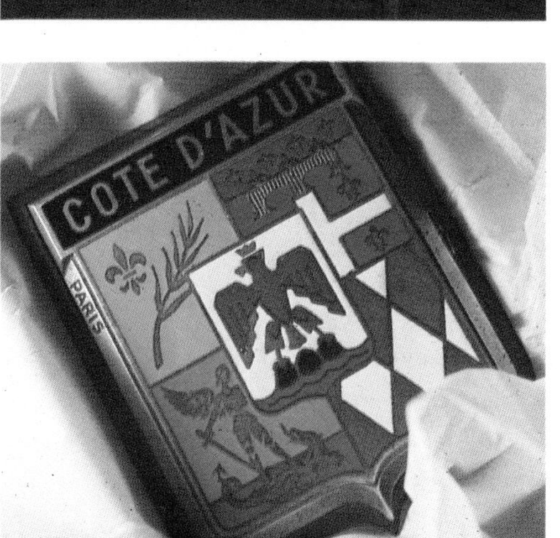

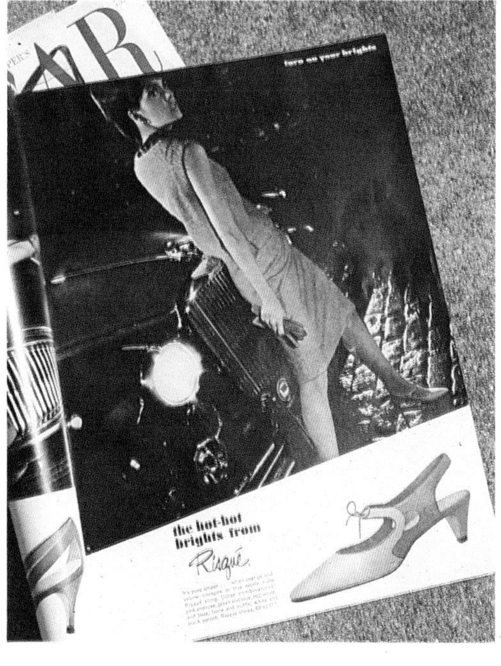

We found a very nice apartment on the 17th floor of 1360 Lake Shore Drive. Genevieve resided 19 floors below, on the lower level of the split level garage. In the lease the space was referred to as 'Stall number 202'. Imagine! We preferred to call it 'Suite 202' out of respect for Genevieve's pride.

From 1964 until we sold Genevieve six years later, a few interesting things occurred. Some of them had a direct, or indirect bearing on our decision.

In 1965, Joan and I spent three weeks touring Europe, a trip we'd planned for a long time. We returned with items for ourselves as well as our families. Of course, Genevieve was not forgotten. She got a plaque from the Cote d'Azur.

However, the most important event of this period had little to do with Genevieve. Roxanne Marie arrived on the scene and, quite naturally, our future activities centred around her, so Genevieve gracefully took a back seat. *Ooopps* .. no pun intended!

In 1967, Genevieve emerged from private life to co-star in a series of ads for The Brown Shoe Company called 'Turn on your brights', and was seen in many of the best magazines. Of course this important role made her unbearably uppity for a while.

* * *

How many kids have a birthday party in the back seat of a car? Not too many, I'll bet, but Roxanne did. She and two friends, and where else but at MacDonalds – Genevieve seemed to enjoy it too.

By 1970 the garage rent had gone up. Insurance rates had soared. Maintenance and repair bills mounted as Genevieve grew older. Many of our friends in the city did not own automobiles as it was much more economical to rent one when needed. All things considered, it seemed a sensible decision to sell Genevieve. We did. All that remained to remember her by was the Genevieve Memorial Wall and portable bar ....

I guess I'd always regretted the decision to sell Genevieve and so, about a year later, I phoned the original buyer in Michigan City, Indiana, and asked him to let me know if he ever contemplated selling the car. I made several of these calls over the years and each time he assured me he would.

By May of 1976 I'd made up my mind, I was definitely going to buy Genevieve back. My wife agreed and so I called again. I couldn't believe it when he told me he had sold the car several months before. I was lucky. He had sold it to a friend of his in nearby Laporte.

I wasted no time in calling the new owner and told him I wanted to buy the car back. He said he would not sell the car, but I was welcome to come over and look at it if I wished. I chose Memorial Day to drive there, cheque book in hand, and full of hope.

I had of course expected to find Genevieve looking as I had last seen her, despite the years that had rolled by, so it was a terrible shock to see her in such deplorable condition. Now my mind was really made-up! I was not going to let a grand and dignified lady like Genevieve come to such a horrible end: not after all the fun times we'd shared. I'd get her back alright, and she'd soon look as good as new.

I patted Genevieve on her bonnet, assured her she'd soon be home where she belonged and headed for the house.

I introduced myself and, after exchanging a few pleasantries, came to the point. Once again I heard the car was *not* for sale. I thought to myself, *car?* That's no ordinary car out there, that's Genevieve! That's ten of the best years of our lives out there! That car is Beekman Towers! That car is Elkart Lake! That car was loved, and pampered and shown, and won, in *Concours*. That car is Toronto! That car is Aunt Mary and the Canadian Winter Rally! That car is social events and laughter and dinners and drinks! That car is Northern Dancer and the Cote d'Azur! That car is Roxanne and MacDonalds! That car! That *car* indeed!

I settled in for a long afternoon.

We did have one thing in common. He was a graphic designer, and so was I. However, I had never attempted to design a house; he had. It was a contemporary house but done with a good deal of warmth that set it apart from the ordinary. We sat in the still-to-be-completed kitchen and, over a few beers, discussed automobiles, the new puppy, houses and the cost of building. The owner and his wife told me they were waiting to buy some very expensive kitchen cabinets. That was it. I made them an offer. They said no. I doubled it, which took them off guard. They huddled in another room for a few minutes, then returned to say no again. I told them I'd go as high as I could and named a figure. Again they went off to the other room. They were gone a long time. Finally they returned. Yes, they'd accept the offer. My hand literally trembled as I wrote out the cheque.

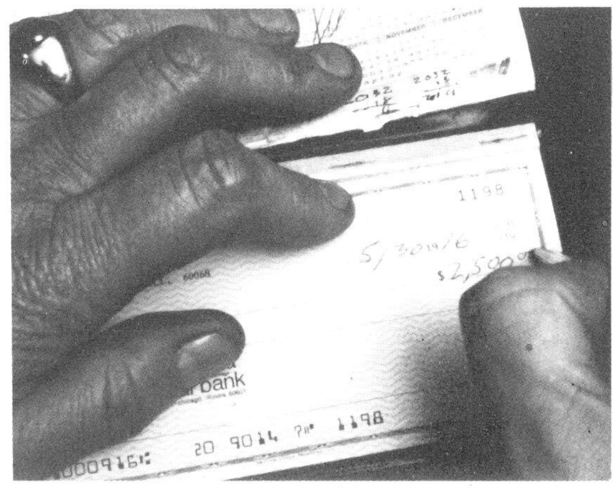

I left the house late that afternoon. I stopped and told Genevieve what had happened, and started back down the long driveway. I was emotionally drained. I stopped again and looked back at Genevieve. Our Genevieve. There were tears in her eyes. Look closely. You can see them ... can't you?

By 1976 home was back in the suburbs. Children have a way of growing up, and Roxanne was no exception. We wanted room for her to play outside and so here we were. When we purchased the house we had no intention of ever owning two automobiles and so the one car garage was not a consideration. Now it became a problem but, like Scarlett O'Hara in *Gone with the Wind,* I'd worry about that later. The important thing now was to get Genevieve home.

Genevieve's last owner had told me he drove the car from Michigan City to his home, but that the brakes were all but non-existent. He also told me that there was a good mechanic in Laporte who, given the time to get the necessary parts, could fix the brakes. That done and a new set of tyres and I could drive her home. Arrangements were made to have Genevieve towed to the garage the following week. On Monday, I called the garage. They had looked at the brakes but it was too big a job for the size of their operation. The only thing to do was somehow get the car to Chicago and find someone there to do the work.

I hardly expected to have someone fall in my lap, but that is about the way it happened. I got a call in the middle of the week from my next door neighbour. He was in the process of opening an auto repair shop, doing body work as well as mechanical. He asked if I would handle his advertising and design. It was all too much, I told him I'd be happy to and when he heard about my car, nothing else would do but that he undertake the work.

The following evening over a few cold beers the person who would do the body work, Bill, my neighbour George, and I, looked at the slides I had taken, agreed to a price and decided to proceed. George already had plans for rapid expansion and restoring an automobile like Genevieve would give excellent publicity.

June 16th was a beautiful sunny day. Bill and I rented a trailer early in the morning and headed for Laporte.

We located the garage, loaded Genevieve aboard the trailer, secured her and set off again back towards Chicago.

Through the back window, I watched Genevieve rolling down the highway once again. She may not have been under her own power, or even on her own wheels, and she did look tacky indeed, but she seemed mighty pleased all the same.

We arrived in Chicago just ahead of the rush hour traffic, roared under the spaghetti-like network of interchanges and overpasses, past the skyscrapers and on to the Kennedy Expressway.

I turned and looked at Genevieve again. She was grinning from headlamp to headlamp! She was back in the big city where she belonged, and did she ever know it!

And so the restoration of Genevieve began. If I had known then what I know now. The time it would take. The money involved. The endless waiting. The frustration of trying to find out who could do what and when. Where do I find this? Where do I find that? Is a part still being made? If not, where can I have it made? Would I have gone through with it? The answer of course is yes, but a qualified yes to be sure. The history and the nostalgia associated with this one particular automobile are the only reasons I saw it through to the end.

Well, I didn't know what the future held and so I was eager to begin and even though I couldn't do the body or mechanical work, there was a great deal I *could* do. The entire interior, as I indicated earlier, was a shambles. All the wood and leather had to be refinished and new carpeting obtained and installed. When I told Joan I intended to do this kind of work myself, she simply smiled and gently reminded me of the bathroom I'd painted in the old apartment that had to be re-done professionally. Well ... this was no bathroom, this was Genevieve, and I was determined to take my time and do a good job.

I took the following week off and arrived at the garage early on Monday. By the end of the day all the interior wood trim, with the exception of the dashboard and the cabinet attached to the back of the front seat, had been removed. Also the small ashtrays in the doors, sun visors, rear view mirror, hub caps, old club badges, the tool compartments that are recessed in each of the two front doors, the radio and lots of other stuff.

Thirty-seven pieces in all, and that was just the beginning ... You have no comprehension of the incredible number of parts that are put into a car interior until you take them out. I took them all home and carefully laid them out in my basement studio.

I decided to start work on my old club badges. Two of the original four had survived. The Oakville Trafalgar Light Car Club and the Canadian Automobile Sports Club. Memories of the little club in suburban Oakville prevailed and so that's where I began. A small start to be sure but an exciting one to me.

I got out my trusty can of Brasso and soaked the badge overnight. The next morning all the encrustations of age had gone and, with them, all the enamel!

I spent many hours restoring this single badge with a number 1 sable brush: it turned out beautifully ... much better than that old bathroom!

The four ashtrays were dirty and rusted. I took them apart, sanded down the metal and sprayed them with silver paint, cleaned their leather coverings with Lexol, and that was that. The tool compartments and the tools inside proved to be more difficult. I soaked the tools overnight in oil and they turned out great. I took the tool compartments themselves and disassembled them, then repainted them in black. The foam rubber padding on the lids had rotted away and so was painstakingly replaced. Many hours later the units looked like new.

So far, so good. A lot of little things remained to be done but two jobs loomed large on the horizon. The wood and the leather. The leather was badly dried out, but, worst of all, there were two large cracks at the top of the front seat. I had no idea what to do about those – so I decided to start on the wood.

The wood actually looked a lot worse than it was. Much of the varnish flaked off to the touch and what did not was still easily removed. I very carefully sanded all the pieces and stored them in my studio. I had not yet chosen a method of refinishing them.

The wood that remained in the car turned out to be another story. These pieces were hard to do and it took hours to just remove the old varnish and sand the wood to a satin finish.

My vacation ended before I could get it all done. I would have to wait until the following weekend to resume my work.

I arrived at the garage early Saturday morning and immediately panicked. All four doors were gone! The interior was gone! I raised the hood to make sure I had an engine ... I did. Suddenly I got the distinct impression that this was going to be more of an undertaking than I had thought. Bill confirmed my impression and my worst fears.

He said the doors could be saved but if somehow we could find new ones we'd be a lot better off. This was true of the front fenders (wings) as well. The rear portion of the body seemed solid, but the body panels beneath the doors were all but non-existent. The rear wheel spats were too far gone to be repaired. All this was but a glimpse of what lay ahead ... The roof and bonnet were fine!

I left the garage and drove to Imperial Motors in the suburb of Wilmette. The chap in the parts department told me that Mk IX parts were no longer being produced, but perhaps the distributor in Indianapolis, Indiana, might have some stored in his warehouse. A phone call soon proved otherwise.

Where to go from here?

I was to find out that there does exist a 'never never land', a land of Jaguar enthusiasts and a land wherein reside the purveyors of elusive and exclusive replacement parts. The names of these purveyors of exotic parts were unknown to me at the time but, over the months, I came to know them well, especially Jo Maletsky.

In the beginning, however, Jaguar in New York seemed to me to be the most logical place to start, probably because that's where it all began so many years ago.

I talked to a most sympathetic chap who simply confirmed what I had found out from Imperial Motors in Wilmette. He did however tell me to get in touch with a shop called Motorcraft Ltd in East Rutherford, New Jersey. If anyone could help me he was sure they could and, indeed, they did.

'Motorcroft' answered the young lady in a very proper British voice. I later found out that she was the wife of the owner and her name was Jackie Maletsky. Her husband's name was Jo. He did not have a proper British voice, but what he did have were many of the parts I needed: I dealt with Jo throughout the entire restoration.

I truly believe that had I trailered Genevieve 900 miles east to Motorcraft, I would have saved a great deal of money and time, not to mention an endless amount of frustration.

At any rate, yes, Jo did have four new doors. He had a left side rocker (sill) panel but not a right. Nor did he have fenders (wings). He asked me if I would like an original equipment air-conditioner. You bet I would. If I remember correctly he said all of these parts had come from a Jaguar Mk IX that developed an electrical fire at a Manhattan dealership years ago, and had just recently surfaced.

I called Bill and told him the news. Towards the end of the week he called back. He came up with the idea of driving a truck to New Jersey and perhaps picking up additional parts he might see there. At the time it seemed like a good idea. However, as it turned out, although he did get a few additional parts, the expense of the trip added up to a cool $700 and I suspect I could have had the parts delivered to Park Ridge for a lot less.

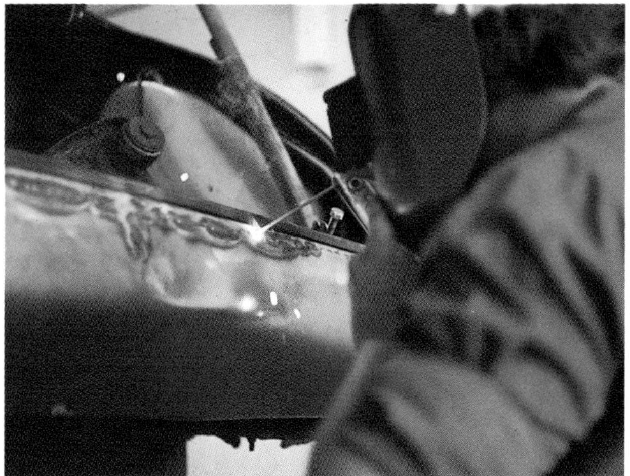

One Saturday morning much to my amazement, I found Genevieve inside the garage. It was probably the first time Genevieve had a roof over her head in five years. Curiosity had got the better of the mechanic and he wanted to check the engine's condition. Boy, did I ever want to as well. Over the ten years I'd owned Genevieve I had adhered religiously to the maintenance schedule and it paid off. Genevieve roared to life. She didn't exactly purr like a kitten, in fact she sounded more like a lion with a bad cold. What matter, the engine was basically fine.

Until now it had not occurred to me to look at the odometer. When I did I got quite a shock. It read 83,393 miles – in five years, Genevieve could not have been driven for more than 1000 miles. Good news indeed.

Body restoration started about the last week in June, 1976. The new doors went on, and the old carpet came out. The fenders (wings) and grille were removed and some body repairs were initiated.

Things started off reasonably well but wound up a shambles. Week after week went by along with excuse after excuse and promise after promise. Genevieve was constantly the one to be pushed aside when the garage was busy.

I figured my money was just as green as anyone else's, so it was really getting to me. However, on October 9, Bill left my neighbour's garage and opened one of his own a mile or so away. I was told that Genevieve would be first in line at the new garage – some work was done, but Bill's preoccupation with dragsters and funny cars, somewhat curtailed at my neighbour's garage, now became paramount. By December 1, I'd had it up to the neck and started looking for another place to take Genevieve. Besides, she really didn't care much for her strange looking companions; after all she was a thoroughbred.

Months before a friend had mentioned a place called Ridge Auto Body in another suburb, Evanston. After visiting the shop and liking what I saw, as well as Steve Pinkerton, the owner, Genevieve was moved there in the middle of January. I might add, her companions at this establishment were of a much more suitable type.

During the six months I'd had Genevieve back, little truly constructive work had been done to her body or mechanical parts. Such was not the case at home. Genevieve's entire interior was stored in my basement within weeks of getting her back and, as I mentioned earlier, the small wooden pieces were all sanded and put away. At this point I had not had time to renovate the large walnut cabinet with the pull down tables that is attached to the back of the front seat, so that is where I began. Within a week, it too was sanded to a satin smooth finish. That was it. All the wood trim was now ready to be brought back to its original warm burled walnut beauty.

The next step really scared me: if the reader wishes to know why, simply do the following. Stop in at your friendly Rolls-Royce dealer and whilst sitting in the driver's seat, bend down so that you are eyeball to eyeball with the instrument panel (the salesman will probably think you're some sort of a nut, but that's okay). What you will see is a mirror image of yourself reflected from the burled walnut finish. No flaws, no brush strokes, no nothin'; just a perfect mirror image. That's what scared me. All I could picture in my mind's eye were little old white-haired men at the Jaguar factory. Men with years of experience who had worked their way up from apprentice to journeyman to master craftsman. These were the sort of people who could do this kind of work. How on earth was I going to match their standards?

I inquired for quite some time as to how to accomplish this. There were a number of alternative ways, but polyurethane varnish seemed to be the overwhelming choice. I still worried about those brush strokes. I was ready to give it a go when I ran into a man at the office who had just completed refinishing the wood on his old Mercedes. The product he used was Formby's Tung Oil and was applied by using one's little pinkie or a cloth. That sounded good. His car was in the office garage and so we went downstairs to see it. I was disappointed when I saw it. It was not a mirror finish, but it was very smooth. My spirits were quickly picked up when he told me the degree of gloss is a matter of choice. The more coats of Tung Oil applied, the higher the gloss. I decided to try it.

I started with the door capping, which is the largest of the trim pieces. I applied coat after coat, carefully wet sanding between each. From the sixth coat on the gloss began to appear.

Eight coats went on, nine, ten, eleven. The twelfth coat did it. When I looked at it after it dried I could have easily been eyeball to eyeball with that Rolls-Royce instrument panel!

Over the months all the pieces were restored to their original, warm burled walnut finish.

If the thought of restoring the wood scared me, the thought of restoring the leather terrified me. The burled walnut was only a small portion of Genevieve's interior. The leather seats, door panels, posts, back window ledge and other pieces were far more apparent to the eye. I took photographs of the dried out leather and two deep cracks along the top of the front seat. I showed them to several interior shops and the answer was always the same. They need to be replaced. Somehow, that did not seem right to me. Those seats were a part of Genevieve. Every bit as much as the engine and the dashboard: they were going to stay, and that was that.

My next stop was Kroch's and Brentanos, a large Chicago bookstore chain. Sure enough, there in the automobile section, along with dozens of other books, was one on interior restoration. I leafed through it and soon realized it was very technical. In fact I read the section on restoring a headliner, something that eventually would have to be done, and almost put the book back. Fortunately I did not. I found the chapter about leather restoration. If the process described by the author worked as well as he said it would, Genevieve's original seats would remain.

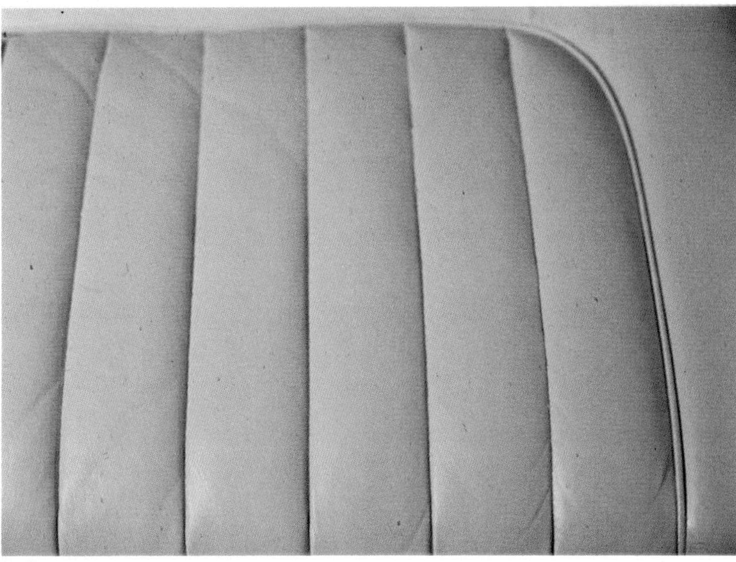

The process recommended was a kit manufactured by The Clausen Co. of Fords, New Jersey. A three step process called 'Leatherique'. I sent for the literature.

By return mail, I received a book along with a ton of testimonials including one very complimentary article in *The Flying Lady,* the monthly magazine of the Rolls-Royce Owners Club.

The booklet described various types of leather and how the work was done at the factory. It then went on to describe how old leather can be brought back to its original softness and how one of the professional methods of colouring leather can be applied to bring back the original pigment of older leather. It went on to say that a wide variety of colours were available; however, if one wished to match the original colour, snip a small piece of leather that was not exposed to the elements and attach it to the order. Remembering the tan *versus* biscuit affair, I did just that and sent off my order.

A week later the kit arrived, C.O.D. $46.50. It contained three cans of liquid and one can of crack filler along with sandpaper and a good quality two-inch paintbrush. The cans of liquid were a cleaner, a rejuvenating oil of some kind, and the Leatherique itself.

Carefully following the instructions, I applied the cleaner with a cloth to remove the dirt and grime, sanding lightly between applications with 180 grit sandpaper.

Having completed that, the rejuvenator oil was the next step. This I applied with the brush they supplied. The oil was allowed to dry overnight. The seats were still very brittle, so I applied a second coat as recommended. The following morning the leather was soft as new. I was delighted beyond words.

In total fairness to The Clausen Co. I must explain fully what I did next. That was to fill those two huge cracks at the top of the seat. The crack filler is meant to be used to fill small cracks on non-pliable surfaces such as door panels or the rear window ledge, and not the way I used it but it worked and it worked well. Not perfectly, but far better that I expected. It took weeks of applying layer upon layer but when the seats were completed, all that showed were two hairline cracks, and that only because it is a pliable surface.

All was now ready for the final step, the Leatherique itself. This also is applied with a brush. The thought of brush strokes still worried me, but the literature assured me none would show. Well, they did show. Try as I might, I could not get rid of all of them. The finish was very glossy and did not look great. To boot, the colour was too light. I finished the first section and went upstairs feeling none too happy. I opened a can of beer and sat down to watch the second half of the Chicago Bears *v* Minnesota Vikings game. After watching Fran Tarkentin march down the field to win the game in the last 18 seconds, I was really in a lousy mood.

I went back down stairs to see how the seat had turned out. I simply could not believe my eyes .... The colour was perfect ...the brush marks had disappeared and the satin sheen finish was beautiful!

A month later all the leather was restored and all I can do is add my endorsement to an incredible product. Thanks, Clausen.

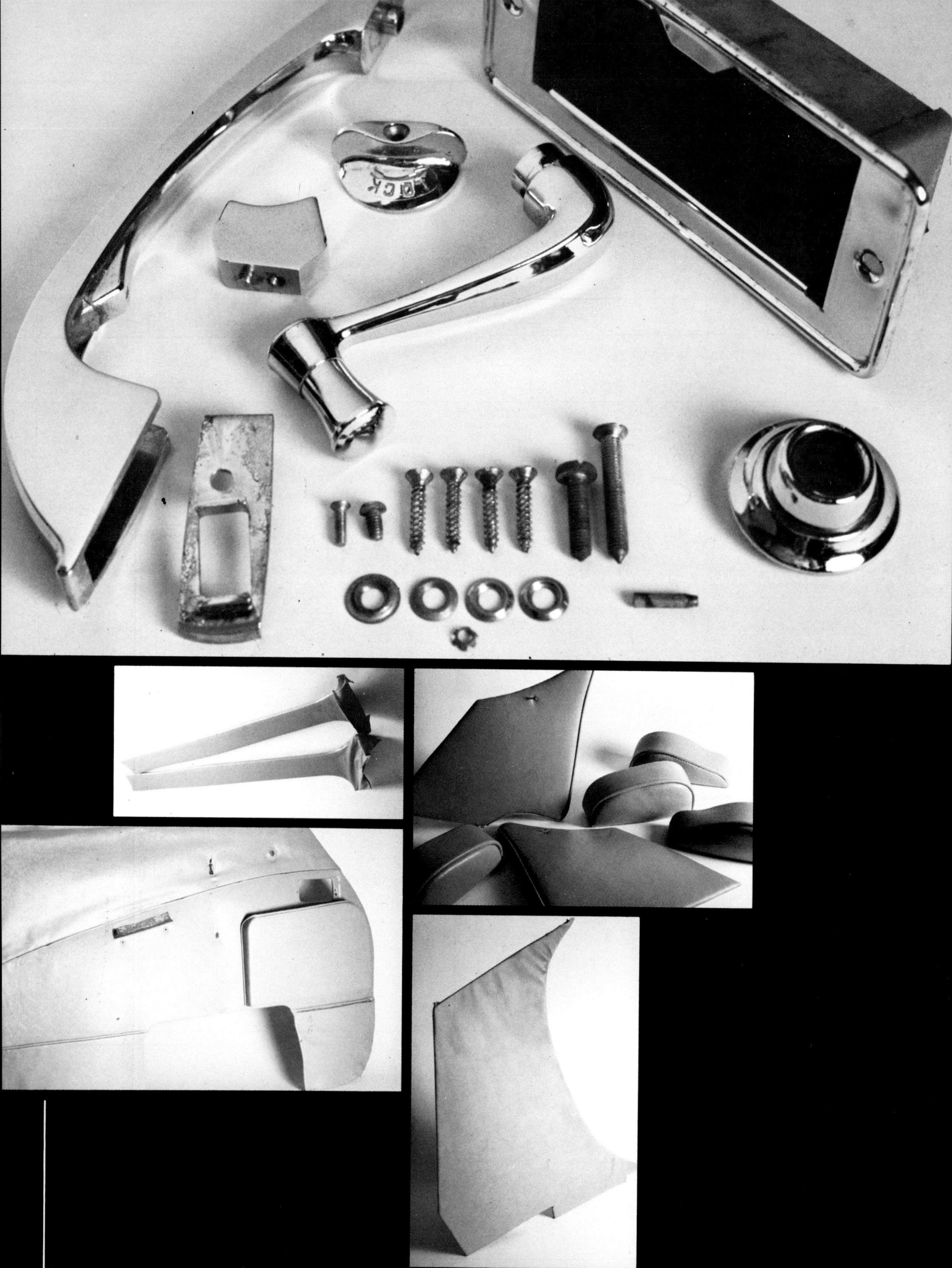
LOCK

Leatherique was applied to the four door panels, the centre posts, armrests and other small leather parts so as to match the colour of the seats. The interior chrome cleaned up well with chrome polish and, by early January 1977, the interior of Genevieve was nearly complete. There remained only one more thing to do. A fun thing. The cabinet between the two pull down tables had always been of little use and so ...

I made it into a mini-bar. I doubt it will get any more use than it has in the past, but it *will* be a conversation piece.

Seven months had passed since the body work on Genevieve had begun and then ground to a halt. The interior was now finished and stored in my basement but, two miles to the west, Genevieve herself remained a shambles.

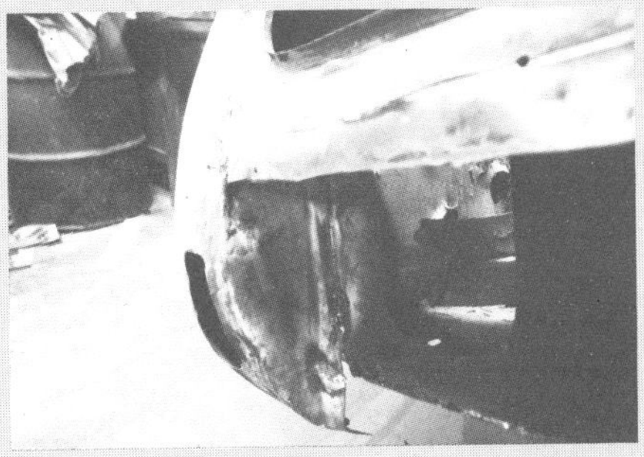

On January 22, 1977, Genevieve was moved to Ridge Auto Body and there the real work began.

It was not my intent when I started this story to go into the technical aspects of the restoration and so I will not. The photographs should suffice to indicate the extent of the work.

Steve Pinkerton, the owner, had estimated the job would take the better part of three months to complete. I was disappointed as I had hoped to have the car by Easter. Aunt Mary was now a spry 87 and still having those two 'shooters' every night. I wanted to surprise her and drive her to Mass on Easter Sunday. That was now out of the question but I didn't know just how out of the question it really was. As it turned out I wouldn't even be able to drive her to Mass the following Easter! It took over two years before Genevieve was finished! The Marriott Corporation built a 1243 room hotel, on Michigan Avenue, in less time.

Why so long? Simple. Economics. All auto body stops have their day-to-day work which cannot wait and so, no matter how well intentioned they may be, a car such as Genevieve takes a back seat. Some of the other delays had causes which stretch belief.

We ordered a rear quarter panel from Jo Maletsky in New Jersey. The east coast was buried in snow along with the Mk IX Jo was cutting up as a donor car. Finally the snow melted and the car was brought inside, cut up and the part shipped. A second storm roared out of the west, stranding all the traffic on the Pennsylvania Turnpike, the truck carrying my quarter panel amongst them.

Two front fenders (wings) were lost for a month, only to be discovered on a loading dock in Youngstown, Ohio. It was nuts!

I ordered five new tyres from a company that shall remain unnamed. Finally, after two months went by, I called to see what had happened. The salesman who had taken my order was on vacation, fortunately for him. I spoke to another man who told me the tyres I had ordered had not been made in ten years! And so it went ... absolutely nutty.

As is obvious from the photographs, most of the work centered around the lower portions of the car. These areas had to be completely rebuilt. The rear quarter panel had to be renewed. The right hand rocker (sill) panel, which I had never been able to find, had to be made from scratch. Myland Suess the man who did all the work on Genevieve is truly an artist with metal. The fenders (wings) finally found their way to Evanston and were fitted on after practically being rebuilt. The radiator was sent out to be rodded. The two fuel tanks (both had holes in them) also went out for repair and so it went, on ... and on ... and on.

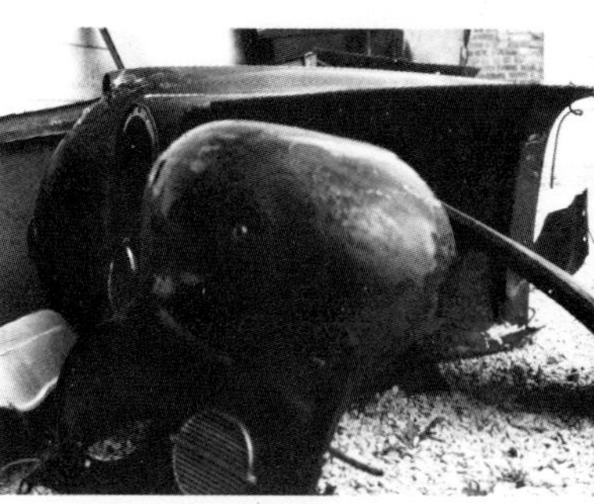

At this point in time, I still had high hopes of getting Genevieve by late summer or early autumn. Therefore, the time had come to make a suitable home for her. Suite 202, her old home on Lake Shore Drive was a nice one to be sure but now that I owned my very own garage, I decided to do something really nice.

The first thing to do was get rid of the bicycles, lawn mower, clay pots, garden chairs and all the other things that find their way into suburban garages. I had a small shed built adjacent to the garage, painted it white and that was that. It looked nice and accomplished the purpose.

My first thought was to panel the whole garage but, after prowling through a whole lot of lumber yards, I thought better of the idea. The real wood panelling cost a small fortune and the cheap stuff looked phoney. At my wife's suggestion, I took a good look at the wood the garage was made of. I washed off a small section and to my amazement, it turned out to be knotty pine. The real stuff!

Two coats of polyurethane later, the walls were a beautiful, rich brown. The Genevieve Memorial Wall, pictures and trophies were moved from the den to the garage. Upon Genevieve's return, she would indeed have a suitable home. The job was finished two days before Memorial Day 1977. One full year had passed since I got Genevieve back.

Several weeks later the new badge bar I'd ordered from California arrived and it was with a great deal of pride and a feeling of satisfaction that I attached each badge. These were the first pieces I'd restored, now nearly a year ago.

The weeks passed by, one after another, and with them went the beautiful driving weather. I kept on checking the progress. Finally, by mid-July it became apparent that Genevieve was nearing completion. The time had come to find a good mechanic to do the required mechanical work.

Myland Suess, the man doing the body restoration, mentioned a friend of his who had a shop in Northbrook, a suburb to the north of Evanston. Not only did he do mechanical work, he did interiors in a separate building. That sounded great since I had no idea of how to install the carpeting I had ordered or how to refit the seats, door panels and all the other things that had to be done. The garage owner's name was Bill Palmer.

The name was not immediately familiar to me, but when I mentioned it to Joan she said it rang a bell. After some thought, she remembered that Bill Palmer had been the owner of a service station in Wilmette, another Chicago suburb. The station has long since been torn down and replaced by a Kentucky Fried Chicken franchise but ... Bill Palmer was the man who had serviced the original Genevieve, the little red XK 120. That was twenty-one years ago!

When I arrived at Northbrook, I recognized him at once. His hair had turned grey but then so had mine. We talked about the old Wilmette service station and he did remember the little 120. He showed me around the garage and the interior shop, introducing me to some of his key people. It was really a big operation. I had little doubt that his shop would do a great job. I told him the car was almost ready and he said to call when it was and he would pick it up.

On August 5 I got a call from Steve. Genevieve was ready to paint!

Seven coats of British Racing Green lacquer were applied. Between every other coat she was wet sanded by hand. After the seventh coat was dry she was polished out and detailed and finally hand buffed to a beautiful lustre.

It took six weeks to complete the job and so, on the morning of September 22, I arrived at Steve's, Genevieve was outside the shop waiting for me. Some chrome was missing and on order from New Jersey but that was a minor item. It was hard to believe that this was the same Genevieve I'd seen sixteen months ago, there in the weeds, her tyres caked with mud, her body rusted and her chrome pitted. But ... that was sixteen months ago and today was today, and today Genevieve looked beautiful!

The first part of the restoration was complete. All the frustration and delays were forgotten. It was time to begin the second phase of the operation, the mechanical work, but little did I know what lay ahead ....

I called Palmer and told him the good news, Genevieve was ready. Bill told me the bad news, he wasn't! It would be at least three weeks before he could get to her and he had no room to store her until then. There was no way Steve could keep her and I was really in a bind, not to mention disappointed. The only thing I could think to do was have her towed back to my house and keep her until Bill could take her. Steve had a suggestion: the mechanic who does the work on his E-type Jaguar was only a block away. It made sense and so Steve called Graham Bowkett at the British Motor Car – I had to admit the company name had a nice ring to it. Yes, Graham could take the car and so I walked over and introduced myself to Mr. Bowkett. He seemed to be a very pleasant chap with a very British accent. He showed me around his garage which was immaculate and housed a number of beautiful machines in various stages of disrepair. I got the impression that Graham would do a good job and so the next morning Genevieve was pushed a block to British Motor Car and work commenced.

I arrived at British Motor Car early the following Saturday. The timing was perfect. All the necessary parts needed to fire up the engine had arrived and were in place. The mechanic was busy working on the fuel pumps which refused to deliver fuel to the proper place. From the questions I asked, I guess he could tell how knowledgeable I was about mechanics, so, when he asked me to assist him, I was delighted. My job was to turn the ignition key on and off when he asked – not too heavy but I performed well. On the tenth try Genevieve roared to life. After running it for five minutes or so, he told me what I had hoped to hear. The engine sounded good, the oil pressure was fine and a compression test would be done soon which he was also sure would be fine. Despite all the rotten treatment Genevieve had endured over the past five years, my attention to the prescribed maintenance schedule had paid off.

To avoid asphyxiation and deafness, future work would have to wait until the mufflers were installed. That sounded reasonable. The muffler system had been made by Motorcraft in New Jersey months ago and the parts were in the luggage compartment of the car. All was progressing as rapidly as I had hoped.

The first week in October the mufflers were neatly laid out on the floor behind Genevieve. The first week in November the mufflers were still neatly laid out on the floor behind Genevieve! Why? One pipe would not fit. But why a month's delay? Anyhow, since Jo Maletsky in New Jersey was familiar with the system I asked Graham to call him. When the problem was explained, Jo immediately knew the solution – wouldn't you know it? The exhaust system on Genevieve was slightly different from most other Mk IX's. It was from the beginning of the transition period from Mk IX to the soon-to-come Mk X ... but why me?

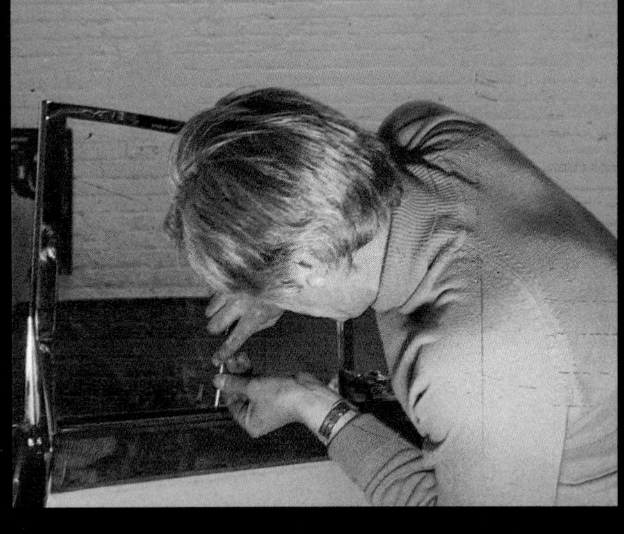

JAGUAR

While we waited for the muffler pipe to arrive, there were other things that could be finished. The interior parts had been finished months ago, the wood, leather and chrome fittings. The exterior chrome that had been lost had been replaced by Motorcraft in New Jersey from their donor car. I had had the parts re-chromed in Chicago and they were also ready.

I had counted on Bill Palmer to do the installation of the interior and final detailing of the exterior, but since he couldn't, and since I had all the parts, I decided to try to do it myself! The very thought of all those nuts and bolts, pins and clips, cranks and handles terrified me, but I figured I couldn't do too much damage. The following Saturday I began. I worked slowly and carefully and, by the third week in January, I had managed to secure the three long strips of chrome along each side and down the centre of the hood, or bonnet if you prefer. Next, on went the leaping cat hood ornament. Did that ever look neat! Several smaller pieces gave me trouble but finally went into place. The last piece to go on was the Jaguar script. It had been shipped from New Jersey in its raw brass state. I filed off all the rough edges, quickly had it chromed, and on it went.

The next step was to attach the four leather door panels and the armrests. Many of the clips that secure the panels to the doors were rusted and couldn't be re-used. I took one to a large auto supply store and got some similar parts. With a little adapting they worked and all four door panels were secured. The left front armrest went on easily, but for the life of me I could not attach the other three. Finally I gave up. I turned my attention to the door handles and window winder cranks – and attention they took, since I hadn't paid any attention when I removed them over a year ago! With a great deal of patience and experimentation, which is not my long suit, I managed to get them all on with no parts left over and best of all ... they worked.

With the exception of the four door cappings, the wood trim went on with relative ease, although the screw holes in the cappings did not match the holes in the door. Drilling new holes in the heavy gauge steel took a long, long time.

Well, it was done. I had installed all the chrome and the interior with the exception of the seats and carpets. I'd have to have that done by a professional, but none the less, I was darned proud of myself – not to mention amazed!

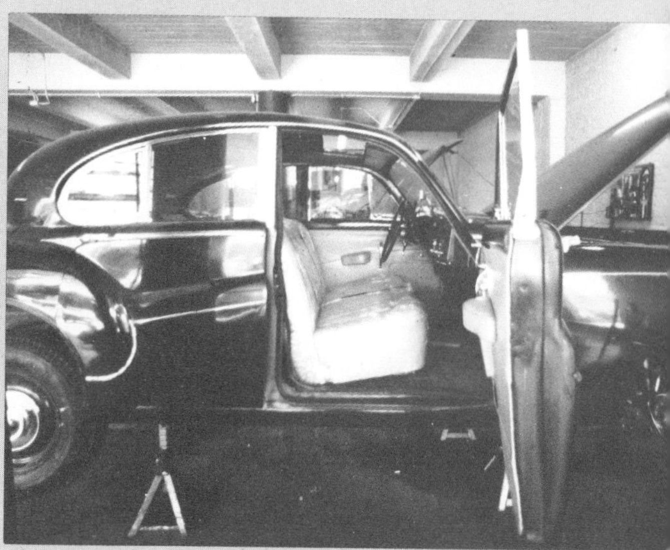

During the time I was installing the interior, the muffler system was put together and work resumed on the engine, wiring, and, by far the most time-consuming and expensive part of the job, the suspension and brakes. Parts for both of these came from all over the United States and Britain. Graham really was doing a fine job.

But, darn it... even considering the complexity of gathering parts, work seemed to be progressing at a snail's pace. April came, then May and along with it the nice weather. Cars came in and went out while Genevieve just sat. Each week I looked at the tools scattered about the base of the car and each week they were in the same position. So was the spanner that rested on the cam covers ....

Finally I'd had it! I called Bill Palmer in Northbrook to see what his situation was. Everything was running smoothly and if I wanted to bring Genevieve up there, come ahead. I phoned Graham and told him that the car was going up to Bill Palmer's place on June 12. If she went up under her own power, fine. If she had to be towed, so be it. Wow! The spanner suddenly disappeared from atop the cam covers and all those other tools were in a different position from then on.

June 11 Graham called to see if he could have an additional day or two. Of course he could. And so, on June 13, I arrived, cheque in hand, to drive Genevieve for the first time in seven years! I didn't! Graham would't accept my personal cheque. I was floored. I'd paid Steve Pinkerton an even larger amount when the body work was completed, and he'd recommended Graham to me. I told him to call Steve, call the bank, anything! No dice. Although to this day I still don't understand this situation, I suppose business men do have their methods of operation and as this was Graham's... so be it. Anyhow, the following morning I arrived at Graham's, gave him a bank certified cheque, fired up Genevieve, and headed for Northbrook.

Seven years! I sat there behind the big steering wheel again, guiding Genevieve under her own power. The seating was high. Left and right fender (wing) tops were clearly visible. At the front of the long tapering hood the big cat mascot atop the radiator seemed to leap forward. I'd forgotten what driving a *real* automobile was like.

I didn't take the expressway. Instead I drove slowly north on the scenic route to Northbrook, along the lake: Genevieve and I had a lot of catching up to do. I do believe that on this trip, Genevieve purred with pleasure – not really surprising when you remember she's a Jaguar. She definitely bristled with pride and self-importance.

By rushing the British Motor Car garage as I had, a few minor, but important, items had been overlooked. Like, if it rained I was in big trouble. The left rear brake light was malfunctioning, the front seat adjusting lever stuck once in a while. Little things. Palmer took care of all these and installed the seats and carpeting. Genevieve remained at Bill's for two weeks.

It had been two years and one month to the day that I patted Genevieve on her bonnet there in Laporte and told her she would soon be home again with us, where she belonged ....

On June 30, 1978, Genevieve came home for good.

– THE END –